Still Looking But Nothing Is Missing

Derrell Lipscomb / *The Rose*

Copyright

© 2026
All rights reserved.

No part of this book may be reproduced, stored, or transmitted in any form without prior permission from the author, except for brief quotations in reviews.

Dedication

For those who sensed something
was true before they could explain
it and were patient enough
to let the unnecessary fall away.

Introduction

*"Truth is what remains
when nothing is propping it up."*

The Rose

Why We Begin

We do not begin the search for clarity because we are confused.

Most people begin because they have experienced **clarity**, however briefly, and recognized it as more real than the state they normally inhabit.

A moment when grief stripped life down to what mattered.
A walk in nature where thought softened and perception sharpened.
A conversation where presence replaced performance.
A period of exhaustion when striving collapsed and something quieter took over.

These moments do not feel artificial.
They feel *honest*.

And once tasted, they introduce a question that does not go away:

Why does this clarity fade?
Why does life become harder again?
What interferes?

This book does not attempt to manufacture clarity.
It does not offer techniques, practices, or promises.

Instead, it examines what **blocks** clarity—and why those obstructions are so persistent, so normalized, and so rarely questioned.

Clarity is not rare.
What obstructs it is common.

And common things are often invisible.

Chapter 1
The Quiet Drift

"We do not see things as they are.
We see them as we are."

Anaïs Nin

Clarity rarely disappears all at once.

It does not usually arrive as a sudden loss, a dramatic collapse, or a moment we can clearly point to and say, *That's when it happened.* Instead, it fades gradually—so slowly that we almost never notice it happening. What was once obvious becomes slightly less so. What once felt simple becomes layered. What once required no explanation begins to feel as though it needs support, justification, or effort to maintain.

This is the quiet drift.

Most people do not wake up one morning confused about their lives. They wake up managing them. They wake up carrying. They wake up already thinking about what must be held together, defended, or navigated before the day has even begun. The sense that something is off often arrives later, as a vague unease rather than a clear problem—an impression that life feels heavier than it should, more complicated than it once did, or strangely distant from a feeling that used to come naturally.

This unease is not a failure of intelligence, discipline, or character. It is not a sign that something essential is missing. More often, it is a sign that something has been quietly accumulating.

The Narrowing of Access

Clarity, when it is present, has a particular quality. It feels open. It feels proportionate. It does not demand urgency or defense. Decisions feel simpler not because fewer options exist, but because fewer distortions interfere with seeing what is already there. There is a sense of alignment—not as an achievement, but as a natural state.

As children, many of us experience this kind of clarity often, though we would not have named it that way. We move toward what interests us and away from what does not without elaborate justification. We feel emotions fully without immediately narrating or managing them. We ask questions because we are curious, not because we are trying to resolve an internal conflict.

Over time, however, layers begin to form.

We learn what is expected of us. We learn which questions are rewarded and which are discouraged. We learn how to explain ourselves in ways that make sense to others. None of this is inherently wrong. Much of it is necessary to function in a shared world. But slowly, almost imperceptibly, the relationship we have with our own perception begins to change.

We stop trusting what we see and feel unless it can be justified.
We stop allowing clarity to stand on its own.
We begin filtering.

The drift does not occur because clarity is fragile. It occurs because access to it narrows under the weight of interpretation, belief, identity, and habit. Like a clear stream that becomes channeled, dammed, or redirected, the water does not disappear—but its movement changes.

What once flowed freely now moves through constrictions.

Accumulation Without Intention

One of the most difficult things to recognize about the quiet drift is that it is rarely intentional.

No one wakes up and decides to obscure their own clarity.
No one consciously chooses confusion as a way of life.

The accumulation happens as a by-product of trying to cope, adapt, belong, succeed, and make sense of uncertainty. We add explanations to stabilize discomfort. We add beliefs to reduce ambiguity. We add identities to anchor ourselves in social systems. Each addition feels reasonable in isolation. Each addition solves a problem—temporarily.

Over time, however, these additions begin interacting with one another. Beliefs reinforce identities. Identities defend beliefs. Explanations multiply to protect explanations. What began as support quietly becomes structure, and what became structure eventually begins filtering perception itself.

The result is not constant confusion. In fact, many people function extremely well within this accumulation. They are competent, thoughtful, capable, and articulate. Yet beneath this functionality there is often a sense of strain—a feeling that life requires more effort than it should, or that something simple has become unnecessarily difficult.

This strain is one of the earliest signals of the quiet drift.

The Feeling of Carrying

Strain does not always announce itself as stress. Sometimes it shows up as mental fatigue, emotional flatness, or a persistent sense of being slightly behind—behind oneself, behind life, behind some unarticulated standard. Sometimes it shows up as restlessness, an inability to fully settle even during moments that are supposed to be restful. Sometimes it appears as overthinking, where even simple decisions feel surprisingly heavy.

These experiences are often interpreted as personal shortcomings: lack of discipline, poor focus, insufficient motivation, unresolved trauma, or the need for improvement. While each of these interpretations may contain partial truths, they often miss something more fundamental.

The issue is not that something essential is missing. The issue is that too much is being carried.

Clarity does not require effort to function. It requires space.

When space is reduced—by constant interpretation, self-monitoring, or internal negotiation—clarity feels distant not because it has left, but because it is crowded.

Why We Don't Notice

If the drift is so consequential, why is it so difficult to see?

Because it happens in the same direction as maturity, responsibility, and adaptation. Many of the changes that narrow clarity are praised by society: being realistic, being careful, being strategic, being consistent, being certain. These qualities are not inherently problematic, but when they become unquestioned defaults, they leave little room for unfiltered perception.

Additionally, the mind is remarkably good at normalizing its own conditions. Whatever state we occupy for long enough begins to feel like "just how things are." The tension becomes background noise. The effort becomes invisible. The constant internal dialogue feels like thinking itself rather than something layered on top of it.

In this way, the quiet drift does not feel like losing clarity. It feels like growing up.

Clarity Is Not Lost—It Is Covered

One of the most important distinctions this book makes is this:

Clarity is not destroyed by accumulation.
It is obscured.

This matters, because what is obscured can be revealed. What is lost must be replaced.

Much of modern self-help, spirituality, and therapy is built around the idea that something essential is missing and must be added back in: confidence, purpose, discipline, healing, enlightenment, or meaning. While these frameworks can provide temporary relief or insight, they often reinforce the same accumulation that caused the obscuration in the first place.

This book takes a different approach.

Rather than asking what must be added, it asks what might be unnecessary.
Rather than seeking transformation, it looks for interference.
Rather than striving for clarity, it examines what blocks it.

This is not a call to abandon responsibility, intelligence, or self-reflection. It is an invitation to notice how much of what we carry is no longer serving perception—and how quietly it has accumulated.

The Return Is Not a Regression

When people hear about subtraction, they often worry that it implies regression: becoming naïve, passive, detached, or less capable. This concern is understandable, especially in a world that equates progress with accumulation.

But clarity uncovered through subtraction does not erase experience. It does not undo learning. It does not return us to childhood. Instead, it allows experience to function without unnecessary mediation.

The clarity that re-emerges is not simplistic. It is seasoned. It carries the depth of lived experience without the burden of constant defense.

This distinction will become increasingly important as we move through the book, especially when we explore contexts where clarity appears spontaneously—during grief, exhaustion, awe, or deep presence. In each of these cases, clarity does not arrive because something new is added. It arrives because something habitual falls away.

An Invitation, Not an Instruction

This chapter does not ask you to do anything.

It does not suggest exercises, practices, or techniques. Those approaches, while sometimes helpful, often introduce new layers of effort and monitoring. Instead, this chapter asks only that you notice.

Notice how clarity feels when it is present.
Notice how effort increases when something is being defended.
Notice how often the mind adds commentary where none is required.

This noticing is not meant to fix anything. It is meant to re-establish a relationship with clarity that has not been gone as long as it may seem.

The quiet drift does not require a dramatic reversal.
It requires recognition.

Once recognized, much of what obscures clarity begins to loosen on its own—not because it is forced to, but because it is no longer necessary.

What Comes Next

The chapters that follow will explore how this accumulation forms, how it maintains itself, and how clarity naturally returns when interference dissolves. We will look at belief, effort, control, and the subtle ways well-intentioned strategies become sources of strain. We will also examine the moments in life when clarity appears without effort, revealing what has been true all along.

But before moving forward, it is worth pausing here.

If something in this chapter resonates—not intellectually, but experientially—that resonance is not something new being introduced. It is something familiar being recognized.

Clarity does not announce itself.
It remains.

And the moment we stop covering it, we begin to see what was never missing.

Chapter 2

Noise, Not Absence

"It is not ignorance but the illusion of knowledge that stands in the way."
— Stephen Hawking

When people say they feel confused, blocked, or lost, they usually describe it as a lack.

Lack of clarity.
Lack of direction.
Lack of motivation.
Lack of confidence.

The language itself points us toward addition. If something is missing, we assume it must be found, learned, healed, or installed. This assumption feels so obvious that it often goes unquestioned. And yet, in lived experience, it rarely holds.

Most moments of confusion do not feel empty.
They feel crowded.

There are too many thoughts, too many interpretations, too many competing signals pulling in different directions. The mind feels busy, not blank. The body feels tense, not inert. Attention fragments not because there is nothing to focus on, but because too much is demanding focus at once.

This chapter invites a simple but radical shift in how confusion is understood.

Confusion is not usually caused by absence.
It is caused by noise.

The Difference Between Silence and Clarity

Silence and clarity are often confused, but they are not the same.

Silence is the absence of sound.
Clarity is the absence of distortion.

A mind can be quiet and still unclear. A life can be full and yet clear. What matters is not the quantity of experience, but how much interference stands between perception and reality.

Noise does not always announce itself as loudness. Often it takes subtler forms: internal commentary, self-evaluation, anticipation, regret, imagined consequences, rehearsed explanations. These layers operate continuously, so continuously that they are mistaken for thinking itself.

When clarity fades, the reflex is to search harder—to analyze, reflect, journal, strategize, or seek insight. Sometimes this helps briefly. Often, it adds another layer of interpretation on top of what was already crowded.

The question this book keeps returning to is not *What do I need to find?*
It is *What is already here that doesn't need to be?*

Everyday Examples of Noise

Consider a simple decision—one that, on the surface, should not be difficult.

You are deciding whether to rest or keep working.

At the level of clarity, the body often already knows the answer. There is fatigue, heaviness, or loss of focus. But before that signal can resolve into action, noise enters:

- *I should be more disciplined.*
- *Other people work harder than this.*
- *If I stop now, I'll fall behind.*
- *Maybe I'm just avoiding discomfort.*

None of these thoughts are inherently false. But together, they obscure the original signal. The decision becomes effortful, strained, and ambiguous—not because the answer is unclear, but because too many voices are speaking at once.

This pattern appears everywhere:

- In relationships, where genuine feeling is buried under analysis and fear.
- In creative work, where inspiration is crowded out by self-monitoring.
- In health, where bodily signals are overridden by narrative and expectation.

In each case, clarity is not absent. It is drowned out.

Why We Add Noise

Noise is not accidental. It is adaptive.

Most internal noise forms as a way to manage uncertainty. When we don't know what will happen, the mind generates possibilities. When we feel vulnerable, it constructs explanations. When we fear loss or rejection, it anticipates outcomes in an attempt to stay safe.

These functions are useful—until they become constant.

Over time, what began as situational coping becomes background operation. The mind continues generating commentary even when no immediate threat exists. The body remains braced even when nothing needs defending. The system stays "on" long after the reason has passed.

This is how noise becomes normalized.

Confusion as a Signal, Not a Failure

If confusion were caused by absence, it would feel empty.

Instead, it feels overloaded.

This is why moments of clarity often arrive not through insight, but through interruption: grief, exhaustion, awe, shock, or stillness. In these moments, noise temporarily collapses. Not because something new appears—but because something stops.

The relief people feel in these moments is often misinterpreted. They say, *I finally found clarity.* More accurately, clarity finally had room.

This distinction matters, because it changes how we respond when clarity fades again. If we believe clarity must be found, we chase it. If we recognize it as ever-present but obscured, we begin noticing what obscures it.

The Cost of Misdiagnosis

When confusion is misdiagnosed as absence, people accumulate solutions.

They collect frameworks, practices, identities, explanations. Each one promises clarity, and each one adds structure. Some help temporarily. Many become new sources of noise.

This is not because the tools are wrong, but because they are applied to the wrong problem.

Noise does not require improvement.
It requires reduction.

Letting the Question Shift

This chapter does not argue against thinking, reflection, or learning. It simply asks that one question be allowed to surface naturally:

What if nothing is missing right now?

This question does not demand an answer. It creates space.

And in that space, something often becomes apparent—not as a thought, but as a release. A sense that effort has been applied where none was required. A recognition that clarity was waiting, unobstructed, beneath the noise.

The chapters ahead will explore the structures that generate and maintain this noise—belief, strain, fixing, and defense—and the contexts in which noise falls away on its own.

For now, it is enough to notice this:

When clarity fades, do not ask what must be added.
Ask what is speaking unnecessarily.

Chapter 3

Belief as a Response to Uncertainty

"Belief is a substitute for experience."
— Joseph Campbell

Belief is often treated as a problem of truth.

We ask whether beliefs are correct or incorrect, rational or irrational, helpful or harmful. We debate which beliefs should be challenged, which should be protected, and which should be replaced with better ones. Entire disciplines are built around refining belief systems, upgrading worldviews, or dismantling faulty thinking.

This chapter takes a different approach.

Rather than asking *whether* a belief is true, it asks *why* the belief appeared at all.

Because belief does not originate in truth-seeking as often as we imagine.
It originates in uncertainty.

What Belief Actually Does

At its core, belief is stabilizing.

When reality feels ambiguous, threatening, or overwhelming, belief provides structure. It organizes perception, assigns meaning, and narrows possibility into something manageable. In this way, belief reduces cognitive and emotional load. It gives the mind something solid to stand on when the ground feels unstable.

This is not a flaw. It is an adaptive response.

The problem does not arise when belief forms.
It arises when belief hardens.

What begins as a temporary scaffold slowly becomes a filter. Over time, belief stops serving uncertainty and starts defending itself. It resists contradiction not because it is true, but because letting go would reintroduce the uncertainty it was built to contain.

This is how belief quietly shifts from support to obstruction.

The Moment Belief Appears

Belief rarely arrives in moments of clarity.

When perception is clear, there is little need to believe anything. Things simply are what they are. Belief enters when clarity wavers—when the future is uncertain, when pain does not make sense, when loss or fear demands explanation.

Consider how often belief forms around moments like these:

- A child experiences emotional unpredictability and forms beliefs about safety or worth.
- An adult encounters repeated failure and adopts beliefs about limitation or destiny.
- A person experiences betrayal and develops beliefs about trust, intimacy, or control.

In each case, belief is not chosen freely. It forms as a way to survive ambiguity.

Belief answers questions that clarity has not yet resolved:

- *Why did this happen?*
- *What does this mean about me?*
- *What should I expect next?*

The answers do not need to be accurate to be effective. They only need to reduce uncertainty.

Belief as Compression

One way to understand belief is as compression.

Reality is complex, fluid, and often contradictory. Belief compresses that complexity into something simpler and more predictable. This compression makes functioning possible, but it comes at a cost.

The cost is fidelity.

Compressed perception trades nuance for certainty. It reduces dimensionality. It filters out information that does not fit the structure it has created. Over time, the world appears increasingly shaped by belief rather than by direct experience.

This is why belief can feel so convincing.
It simplifies.

And simplicity feels like clarity—until it doesn't.

When Belief Becomes Noise

As we explored in the previous chapter, confusion often feels crowded rather than empty. Belief is one of the primary contributors to that crowding.

Not because belief is loud, but because it is constant.

Beliefs operate in the background, shaping interpretation before we are aware that interpretation is happening. They answer questions automatically. They generate expectations reflexively. They frame experience before it has a chance to be experienced.

When multiple beliefs interact—about self, others, work, relationships, health—the noise compounds. Each belief speaks with authority. Each demands consistency. Each resists revision.

The result is not necessarily wrong action, but strained perception.

We begin responding not to what is happening, but to what belief predicts.

The Difference Between Seeing and Knowing

Clarity does not require belief.

This statement can feel unsettling, especially in cultures that equate knowing with believing. But there is a crucial distinction between seeing and knowing.

Seeing is immediate.
Knowing is accumulated.

Seeing does not require defense.
Knowing often does.

When clarity is present, there is no need to convince oneself of what is being perceived. There is no internal argument. There is simply recognition.

Belief enters when recognition feels insufficient—when we want assurance, permanence, or justification.

This is not wrong. But it is revealing.

Why Beliefs Persist

Beliefs persist not because they are true, but because they are functional.

They organize identity.
They create continuity.
They provide a sense of coherence over time.

Letting go of a belief can feel like losing a piece of oneself—not because the belief is essential, but because identity has been built around it. This is why challenging belief often triggers defensiveness rather than curiosity.

Defensiveness is not protecting truth.
It is protecting stability.

This insight changes how belief is approached in this book. The goal is not to attack belief, dismantle it aggressively, or replace it with a superior framework. Doing so often recreates the same problem in a different form.

Instead, the goal is to see belief clearly enough that it no longer needs to be defended.

Belief and the Body

Beliefs do not live only in thought.

They settle into posture, muscle tension, breathing patterns, and habitual responses. A belief about danger may show up as chronic tightness. A belief about inadequacy may appear as inhibition of expression. A belief about control may manifest as constant vigilance.

This is why belief cannot be resolved purely through intellectual insight. Even when a belief is consciously questioned, the body may continue responding as if it were still true.

Later in the book, we will explore this more directly when we address how narratives and trauma are stored in the body. For now, it is enough to recognize that belief is embodied.

And what is embodied cannot be argued away.

The Illusion of Replacing Beliefs

One of the most common responses to problematic belief is replacement: substituting a "better" belief for a limiting one. While this can offer temporary relief, it often reinforces the underlying mechanism.

The structure remains. Only the content changes.

A belief about unworthiness is replaced with a belief about worthiness.
A belief about limitation is replaced with a belief about

potential.
A belief about chaos is replaced with a belief about order.

Each replacement still relies on belief to stabilize uncertainty.

This book does not advocate belief replacement. It points toward something quieter.

When clarity is allowed to operate, belief becomes optional.

What Happens When Belief Loosens

When belief loosens—even slightly—something surprising happens.

Perception widens.
Reactivity softens.
Effort decreases.

Not because answers have been found, but because fewer answers are being demanded.

This loosening does not require force. It begins with noticing—noticing how often belief speaks on behalf of experience, how often interpretation arrives before sensation, how often certainty is used to avoid not knowing.

Not knowing is not the enemy of clarity.
It is its precondition.

An Invitation to Notice

This chapter does not ask you to challenge your beliefs.

It asks you to notice when belief is operating—and what it is responding to.

- What uncertainty is this belief trying to resolve?
- What feeling might arise if this belief were not present?
- What effort is required to maintain it?

These questions are not meant to be answered immediately or conclusively. They are meant to restore contact with experience beneath belief.

Clarity does not require belief to disappear.
It requires belief to stop leading.

What Comes Next

The next chapters will examine what happens when belief hardens into effort, strain, and attempts at fixing. We will explore how control masquerades as responsibility, and how self-support becomes self-interference.

For now, it is enough to see belief not as an enemy, but as a signal.

A signal that uncertainty was present.
A signal that clarity was momentarily inaccessible.
A signal that something was added—not because it was true, but because it was needed.

When belief is seen this way, it no longer needs to be fought.

And when it no longer needs to be fought, it often loosens on its own.

Chapter 4
Effort vs. Strain

"Nature does not hurry, yet everything is accomplished."
— Laozi

Effort is not the problem.

This may come as a relief to some readers and a disappointment to others, but it is essential to say plainly at the outset: clarity does not eliminate effort. Life requires movement, engagement, and action. Growth involves learning. Creation involves work. Care involves attention.

The issue is not effort itself.

The issue is strain.

Strain feels like effort, but it is not the same thing. It carries a different texture, a different cost, and a different signal. Most people know strain intimately, even if they have never named it. It is the feeling of pushing against something invisible, of applying more force than the situation seems to warrant, of working harder while becoming less effective.

Strain is effort applied in the presence of distortion.

And because distortion often goes unseen, strain is usually misinterpreted.

How Strain Becomes Normal

For many people, strain feels synonymous with responsibility.

We learn early that effort is virtuous. We praise persistence, discipline, and sacrifice. We admire those who push through difficulty and continue despite discomfort. These values are not wrong. But when strain becomes the default mode of engagement, it stops being questioned.

Over time, the body and mind adapt to constant strain. Tension becomes familiar. Fatigue becomes background noise. The feeling of "trying" becomes indistinguishable from the feeling of "doing." In this state, the absence of strain can feel suspicious, even irresponsible.

This is how strain becomes normalized.

And once normalized, it becomes difficult to distinguish from effort.

The Felt Difference

Effort has a sense of proportion.

When effort is aligned, it rises naturally to meet the demand and recedes when the demand passes. There is a sense of engagement without contraction, of focus without rigidity. Even when effort is sustained, it does not feel adversarial. There is friction, but not resistance.

Strain feels different.

Strain carries urgency.
Strain carries self-monitoring.
Strain carries a subtle pressure to justify itself.

Where effort feels responsive, strain feels compensatory. It arises not from what is required, but from what is being defended, maintained, or forced into coherence.

Most people sense this difference immediately when it is pointed out. The difficulty is not recognizing strain — it is noticing how often it has become the baseline.

Where Strain Comes From

Strain does not arise from difficulty alone.

It arises when belief, noise, or expectation overlays reality and effort is applied to maintain that overlay.

Consider a common example: performance.

Two people may be doing the same task, at the same level of difficulty, for the same amount of time. One feels engaged and tired in a clean way. The other feels depleted, tense, and pressured.

The difference is not the task.

The difference is what else is being carried:

- the need to prove competence
- the fear of falling behind
- the belief that worth is tied to outcome
- the anticipation of judgment

Effort is being spent not only on the task, but on sustaining an internal narrative around the task. That additional expenditure is strain.

Strain is effort spent defending belief.

Strain as a Signal

Because strain is so often framed as a personal failing — lack of resilience, poor discipline, insufficient motivation — people respond to it by trying harder.

This compounds the problem.

Strain is not a signal to increase effort.
It is a signal that effort is being misapplied.

When strain appears, something extra is present. Something is being held in place that requires continuous force to maintain. The force is not what is exhausting — the maintenance is.

Seen this way, strain becomes informative rather than accusatory. It points not to weakness, but to misalignment.

The Myth of Effortless Living

At this point, it is important to address a common misunderstanding.

Distinguishing effort from strain does not mean seeking a life without effort. Nor does it mean avoiding challenge, discomfort, or responsibility. Those interpretations often arise from belief systems that swing between extremes: either constant struggle or passive ease.

Clarity does not eliminate effort.
It eliminates unnecessary effort.

When distortion falls away, effort becomes more precise. It is applied where it is needed and withdrawn where it is not. This can feel unfamiliar at first, especially for those accustomed to constant striving.

Some people experience guilt when strain decreases, as though something essential has been abandoned. Others feel disoriented by the absence of internal pressure. These reactions are understandable. They reflect how deeply strain has been conflated with virtue.

Strain and Identity

Strain often persists because it has become part of identity.

"I'm someone who works hard."
"I push myself."
"I don't quit."

Again, these are not inherently problematic. But when identity is built around strain, letting go of strain can feel like letting go of self.

This is why relief sometimes triggers anxiety.

When strain loosens, the mind asks: *Who am I if I'm not pushing?*
This question does not indicate a problem. It indicates a transition.

The chapters ahead will explore this more directly, especially when we examine fixing, surrender, and the end of self-support. For now, it is enough to notice that strain is often protected not because it is necessary, but because it is familiar.

Everyday Examples

Strain shows up in subtle, ordinary ways.

In conversation, strain appears as rehearsing what to say instead of listening.
In relationships, it appears as managing impressions rather than being present.
In health, it appears as overriding bodily signals in the name of discipline.
In creativity, it appears as forcing output instead of allowing emergence.

In each case, effort is real — but strain is optional.

When strain falls away, action often becomes more effective with less force. This can feel counterintuitive at first. We are taught that results scale with effort, but in reality they scale with alignment.

Alignment Is Not a Strategy

Alignment cannot be manufactured.

This is crucial.

The moment alignment becomes a goal, it turns into another object of strain. People begin monitoring themselves for signs of ease, judging their experience against an imagined ideal. This adds another layer of effort on top of what was already present.

Alignment arises when interference is removed.

It is a consequence, not an achievement.

This is why the approach of this book remains subtractive. We are not learning how to apply effort more skillfully. We are noticing where effort is being applied unnecessarily.

Listening to Strain Without Fixing It

This chapter does not ask you to eliminate strain.

It asks you to listen to it.

Strain is not asking to be defeated. It is asking to be understood. When strain is noticed without judgment or immediate correction, it often reveals what is being carried beneath it: a belief, a fear, an expectation, a narrative that has quietly taken over the steering.

When that underlying layer is seen, effort naturally recalibrates. Not because it was forced to, but because the reason for strain is no longer present.

What Comes Next

The next chapter will look at what happens when strain is misinterpreted as a flaw and the mind responds by trying to fix itself. We will explore how self-improvement, control, and even surrender can become new forms of interference when they are used to manage strain rather than understand it.

For now, it is enough to leave this chapter with a simple recognition:

Effort that feels clean does not argue with itself.
Strain always does.

And when strain appears, it is not asking for more force. It is asking what no longer needs to be held.

Chapter 5
The Illusion of Fixing

"Trying to change what is… blocks seeing what is."
— Alan Watts

When strain is misunderstood, the instinct to fix appears.

This instinct feels responsible. Even compassionate. After all, if something feels wrong, uncomfortable, or difficult, shouldn't it be addressed? Shouldn't effort be redirected toward improvement, healing, or resolution?

This assumption is rarely questioned.

And yet, much of the strain people carry does not arise because something is broken. It arises because something is being interfered with.

Fixing enters the picture when strain is misdiagnosed as a flaw.

Fixing as a Reflex

Fixing often feels like progress.

When discomfort appears, the mind moves quickly to interpretation:

- *Something is wrong with me.*
- *I need to change this.*
- *I need to work on myself.*
- *I need a better strategy.*

These thoughts arrive so automatically that they are rarely noticed as additions. They feel like responsibility itself. But responsibility, when driven by distortion, becomes another form of strain.

Fixing is not inherently harmful. Many problems do require repair, learning, or intervention. The issue arises when fixing is applied indiscriminately—especially inwardly.

The inner world is not a machine.
Clarity is not a mechanism.
Strain is not a malfunction.

When Fixing Becomes Interference

Fixing becomes interference when it is applied to states that are already self-correcting.

Confusion, uncertainty, fatigue, emotional fluctuation—these are not errors. They are conditions. They resolve naturally when they are allowed to do so. When fixing intervenes prematurely, it often prolongs what it is trying to end.

This is why people sometimes feel worse after trying to fix themselves.

They add:

- analysis on top of feeling
- judgment on top of sensation
- strategy on top of uncertainty

Each addition increases noise.

Instead of asking *What is happening?*
Fixing asks *What must be done about this?*

The first opens perception.
The second closes it.

The Fixer's Loop

Once fixing becomes the default response to strain, a loop forms.

Strain appears → fixing is applied → temporary relief occurs → strain returns → fixing intensifies.

This loop is exhausting because it never addresses the source of strain. It treats symptoms while reinforcing the underlying pattern: the belief that internal states must be managed, corrected, or optimized.

Over time, people begin fixing the fixing.

They seek better frameworks, deeper insight, more precise language, more advanced practices. Each iteration promises resolution. Each iteration adds structure.

What is rarely questioned is whether fixing itself might be the interference.

Self-Improvement as a Form of Control

Much of what passes for self-improvement is, at its core, an attempt to regain control over experience.

Control feels reassuring in the presence of uncertainty. It creates a sense of agency. But when applied inwardly, control often suppresses the very signals that would naturally guide recalibration.

This is why people can become highly skilled at managing themselves while feeling increasingly disconnected.

They are functional, articulate, and disciplined—but effortful.
Capable—but tense.
Improving—but not clearer.

Fixing improves performance.
Clarity improves perception.

They are not the same.

Why Fixing Feels Necessary

Fixing persists because it works—just enough.

It provides temporary relief, a sense of movement, a feeling of doing something. In cultures that equate motion with progress, this is deeply reinforcing.

Stillness, by contrast, can feel irresponsible. Waiting can feel passive. Not intervening can feel like neglect.

But clarity does not emerge through neglect.
It emerges through non-interference.

This distinction is subtle, and it is why fixing is so persuasive. It borrows the language of care while quietly increasing strain.

The Quiet Cost of Constant Adjustment

When fixing becomes habitual, life turns into a series of adjustments.

Feel tired? Optimize.
Feel uncertain? Reframe.
Feel pain? Work through it.
Feel lost? Find purpose.

Each adjustment may be reasonable in isolation. But taken together, they create a constant posture of self-surveillance. Attention turns inward, not to observe, but to correct.

This posture fragments presence.

Instead of being in experience, one stands slightly outside it, monitoring, evaluating, and intervening. The distance is small—but persistent.

That distance is enough to obscure clarity.

Letting the System Settle

Systems that are not interfered with often self-organize.

This is true biologically, emotionally, and perceptually. When interference ceases, tension redistributes. Signals recalibrate. Noise dissipates.

Fixing interrupts this process.

This does not mean that nothing should ever be done. It means that not everything that feels uncomfortable is asking to be changed.

Some states are asking to be felt.
Some questions are asking to remain open.
Some tensions are asking to unwind.

Fixing answers too quickly.

What Comes Next

The chapters so far have examined how clarity becomes obscured through accumulation, belief, strain, and fixing. At this point, a crucial question arises:

If we stop fixing, what happens to what we are carrying?

This is where many people become uneasy. Because not everything that is carried lives in thought. Some of it lives in the body.

And the body does not respond to fixing the way the mind does.

That is where we turn next.

Chapter 6

What the Body Carries

"The body keeps the score."
— Bessel van der Kolk

Not everything that obscures clarity is conceptual.

Some of what interferes with perception is held in the body—quietly, persistently, and often outside of conscious awareness. This holding does not announce itself as belief or thought. It announces itself as tension, inhibition, fatigue, pain, or illness.

The body remembers what the mind has learned to narrate.

Beyond Story

Trauma is often discussed in terms of events and stories. But what remains after an event is not the story itself. It is the bodily response that never completed.

The body contracts.
Breath shortens.
Muscles brace.
Expression halts.

If the response cannot resolve—because the environment is unsafe, overwhelming, or unresponsive—the contraction remains.

Over time, narratives form *around* this holding:

- *I'm not safe.*
- *I shouldn't express that.*
- *I have to stay in control.*

These narratives are not the trauma. They are adaptations built around bodily memory.

The Body as Archive

The body is not symbolic. It is literal.

It does not store meaning. It stores sensation. Tension patterns, breathing habits, posture, and movement restrictions become the living record of what was once necessary.

This is why people can intellectually understand an experience and still feel bound by it. Insight does not automatically reach the level at which the body is holding.

And this is why fixing fails here.

The body does not respond to correction.
It responds to safety.

Health and Expression

When bodily holding persists, it often expresses itself indirectly.

Energy that could move toward expression is diverted toward containment. Voice tightens. Gesture diminishes. Emotion flattens or overwhelms. Over time, systems under chronic tension begin to signal distress through pain, fatigue, or dysfunction.

These signals are not malfunctions.
They are communications.

Attempts to override them—through discipline, optimization, or positive thinking—often deepen the holding.

What the body carries does not need to be solved.
It needs permission to complete.

Subtraction at the Somatic Level

Just as clarity emerges when mental interference is removed, bodily clarity emerges when unnecessary holding is allowed to release.

This does not happen through force.
It happens through presence.

Presence here does not mean analysis or technique. It means allowing sensation without immediately naming, interpreting, or managing it. When sensation is met without demand, the body often begins to unwind on its own.

This is not dramatic.
It is gradual.
And it is precise.

Expression as Resolution

Many people discover that as bodily holding releases, expression changes.

Voice becomes steadier.
Movement becomes freer.
Emotion becomes more proportional.

Not because something new was learned—but because something old was no longer held.

This is why clarity and expression are so closely linked. When the body is no longer bracing, perception clears. When perception clears, expression flows.

No Timeline, No Prescription

This chapter does not offer a method for release.

That would be another form of fixing.

Instead, it offers recognition: much of what feels like obstruction is not a problem to solve, but a signal to stop interfering. The body knows how to resolve what it holds when it is no longer required to suppress it.

This process cannot be rushed.
And it does not need to be directed.

What This Makes Possible

As bodily holding softens, effort recalibrates. Beliefs loosen. Fixing becomes less compelling. Clarity is no longer an abstract state—it is felt.

Chapter 7
Clearing Without Control

"The moment you accept authority, clarity ends."
— Jiddu Krishnamurti

The word *clearing* carries weight.

For some, it evokes moments of unmistakable relief—mental quiet, emotional lightness, a sense of burdens lifting without effort. For others, it carries caution, even alarm, because it has been used within systems that combine insight with control.

Both reactions are understandable.

This chapter exists to make a distinction that is rarely made cleanly:

Clearing is real.
Control systems are also real.
They are not the same thing.

Confusing them has caused harm in both directions—by dismissing genuine experiences, and by granting authority to structures that do not deserve it.

What Clearing Actually Refers To

At its most basic level, clearing refers to the reduction of interference.

When something that was previously obscuring perception falls away, experience feels lighter, simpler, and more direct. Thought quiets. Emotion becomes more proportional. Attention stabilizes without effort.

Nothing new is added.
Something old releases.

This aligns precisely with the core thesis of this book.

Clearing is not an achievement.
It is an uncovering.

It does not require belief.
It does not require ideology.
It does not require permission.

It happens naturally in many contexts:

- after emotional release
- during deep presence
- in moments of exhaustion
- following grief
- sometimes unexpectedly, without explanation

The experience itself is not mysterious.
What *becomes* problematic is how it is framed.

When Systems Discover Clearing

Any system that notices clearing will be tempted to organize around it.

This is not unique to any one movement, religion, or institution. Wherever humans notice that a particular process reliably produces relief or clarity, structure follows. Language forms. Roles emerge. Authority consolidates.

At first, this can appear helpful.

People want to understand what happened to them.
They want to repeat it.
They want to stabilize it.

This is where the risk begins.

Clearing, by its nature, cannot be owned.
The moment it is systematized as an outcome to be delivered, measured, or maintained, it becomes vulnerable to control.

The Subtle Shift From Insight to Authority

The shift is rarely overt.

It begins with explanation:

- *This is why you feel clearer.*
- *This is how it happened.*
- *This is how to continue.*

Explanation feels reassuring. But when explanation hardens into exclusive interpretation, authority quietly enters.

Soon after comes dependence:

- *You need this process to stay clear.*
- *You cannot see this on your own.*
- *Outside influences will undo this state.*

At this point, clearing is no longer about removing interference.
It has become something to protect, defend, and manage.

Which means interference has returned—now institutionalized.

Why Control Can Feel Convincing

Control systems often feel convincing precisely because they are built around something real.

They do not invent clarity.
They discover it.

But instead of pointing back to the individual's own perception, they redirect credit outward—to the system, the method, the authority.

This inversion is subtle.

Instead of:

Clarity emerged because interference fell away.

The framing becomes:

Clarity emerged because this system worked.

Once this shift occurs, autonomy erodes.

Clearing becomes conditional.
Access becomes mediated.
Freedom becomes compliance.

The tragedy is that the original insight—subtraction—gets buried under structure.

The Nugget That Must Not Be Lost

Here is the nugget that must be preserved, even when systems fail:

Clearing does not require control.

The relief people experience in structured clearing environments does not arise from obedience, hierarchy, or ideology. It arises because attention is temporarily freed from narrative, defense, and self-monitoring.

Often this happens through:

- focused attention without interruption
- being listened to without correction
- repeating experiences until emotional charge dissipates
- allowing sensation to complete without suppression

These conditions are not proprietary.
They are human.

Any environment that creates them may produce clearing.
Any environment that claims ownership over them becomes dangerous.

Clearing vs. Dependency

A critical distinction emerges here:

Clearing increases self-trust.
Dependency decreases it.

If a clearing experience leaves someone feeling:

- more capable of seeing for themselves
- less compelled to explain or justify
- less reliant on external validation

It is aligned with clarity.

If it leaves someone feeling:

- dependent on continued intervention
- fearful of losing access
- suspicious of independent thought

Then clearing has been co-opted by control.

This distinction matters more than the label applied to the experience.

Why Clearing Cannot Be Stabilized

One of the most seductive promises made by control systems is permanence.

Stay clear.
Remain at this level.
Protect what you've achieved.

But clarity does not stabilize the way identity does.

Clarity is not a state to maintain.
It is a condition that reappears when interference is absent.

Trying to lock it in place guarantees strain.

This is why attempts to preserve clearing often lead to increased rules, vigilance, and correction. The system senses loss and tightens. The individual senses pressure and complies—or breaks.

Both outcomes miss the point.

Clearing Without Ownership

This book treats clearing as something that belongs to no one.

Not to institutions.
Not to teachers.
Not even to the self as an identity.

Clearing is simply what happens when noise subsides.

The moment it is framed as an accomplishment, it begins to fade.
The moment it is framed as a gift from authority, it becomes distorted.

True clearing leaves no trace.
No badge.
No obligation.

The Quiet Return of Control

It's worth naming one more subtlety.

Even outside formal systems, people often recreate control internally. They try to monitor their clarity, correct deviations, and "get back" to a cleared state. This internalizes the same structure that external systems impose.

The result is self-surveillance.

Clarity becomes another thing to manage.

This book resists that move entirely.

Clearing is not something you do.
It is something that happens when you stop doing certain things.

What Clearing Actually Asks

Clearing asks very little.

It asks for:

- honesty without performance
- attention without agenda
- sensation without narrative
- time without pressure

These conditions cannot be enforced.
They can only be allowed.

And when they are allowed, clearing often occurs on its own—quietly, without ceremony.

What Comes Next

Now that clearing has been separated from control, the book can move forward safely.

The next chapters will explore contexts where clearing happens without systems at all—grief, exhaustion, presence, love, awe. In each case, no one is in charge. Nothing is being delivered. And yet clarity appears.

This reinforces the central insight:

Clarity does not belong to institutions.
It does not belong to methods.
It does not belong to authority.

It remains available wherever interference falls away.

Chapter 8
When Nothing Is Being Defended

"What you resist, persists."
— Carl Jung *(commonly attributed)*

There are moments when something unusual happens.

Nothing dramatic changes. The circumstances remain the same. The situation may still be difficult, uncertain, or unresolved. And yet, something releases. The pressure eases. Thought quiets. The body softens.

It can feel subtle, even easy to miss.

But in those moments, one thing is true:

Nothing is being defended.

The Background Tension Most People Carry

Most people live with a low-level tension they no longer notice.

It is not constant stress or overt anxiety. It is subtler than that. A slight bracing. A readiness to explain. A tendency to justify, anticipate, or protect something—often without knowing exactly what.

This tension accompanies thought, speech, and action. It is present in conversations, decisions, and even moments of rest. It does not announce itself as fear. It announces itself as *management*.

What is being managed is not always obvious.

Sometimes it is an image of competence.
Sometimes a sense of goodness.
Sometimes an idea of being right, safe, reasonable, or in control.

Often it is not a belief that can be articulated at all, but a feeling that must not be disturbed.

This is defense.

Defense Is Not Aggression

Defense does not require opposition.

One can be polite, calm, intelligent, and articulate—and still be defending. Defense is not about fighting others. It is about maintaining internal coherence at all costs.

It appears as:

- explaining when no explanation is required
- correcting before being questioned
- rehearsing responses before they are needed
- feeling subtly threatened by disagreement
- tightening when uncertainty appears

None of these are moral failings. They are adaptive responses that once served a purpose.

But what once protected clarity now obscures it.

What Defense Protects

Defense does not protect truth.

It protects *structure*.

Beliefs, identities, narratives, and self-concepts require maintenance. They must remain intact to feel safe. Defense is the activity that keeps them intact.

This is why defense is effortful.
This is why defense generates strain.
This is why defense resists silence.

When nothing is being defended, effort drops—not because responsibility is abandoned, but because there is nothing left to prop up.

The Moment Defense Falls Away

Defense does not usually dissolve through argument.

It dissolves through irrelevance.

A moment arrives—sometimes quietly—when whatever was being protected no longer feels necessary. The reason for holding tight vanishes. Not because it was disproven, but because it is no longer needed.

This can happen:

- in moments of emotional honesty
- when exhaustion removes the capacity to maintain posture
- when presence deepens beyond self-monitoring
- when loss renders narrative unnecessary

When defense falls away, clarity appears immediately.

Not as insight.
As relief.

The Feeling of Undistorted Perception

When nothing is being defended, perception changes quality.

There is more space.
Less urgency.
Less internal commentary.

Thought still happens, but it does not argue with itself. Emotion still arises, but it does not demand explanation. Action still occurs, but it does not feel pressured to justify its existence.

This state is often described as "being oneself," though that phrase is misleading. It is not a return to a better self. It is the absence of the effort to be something.

Why Defense Is Hard to See

Defense is difficult to see because it is usually justified.

It feels responsible.
It feels protective.
It feels necessary.

And because it often formed in response to real experiences—hurt, loss, misunderstanding—it carries emotional legitimacy.

But legitimacy does not mean permanence.

Defense that once made sense can quietly outlive its usefulness.

The problem is not that defense exists.
The problem is that it is rarely questioned.

Asking the Right Question

This chapter introduces a question that will return again and again in the book:

What is being defended right now?

Not:

- *What do I believe?*
- *What am I afraid of?*
- *What should I do?*

But simply:

- *What is being defended?*

Often, no clear answer appears.

That itself is informative.

More often than not, what is being defended is not a thought, but a sensation—an unease, a vulnerability, a memory that never fully resolved.

Defense exists to keep that sensation from surfacing.

Defense and Expression

Defense restricts expression.

When something is being defended, speech tightens. Voice modulates. Words are chosen carefully. Authentic expression feels risky, not because it is wrong, but because it might disturb what is being protected.

This is why many people feel a gap between what they feel and what they can say.

When defense drops, expression becomes simpler. Not louder or more dramatic—just more direct.

Clarity speaks quietly.

The Paradox of Safety

Defense is meant to create safety.

But over time, it produces the opposite.

Maintaining defense requires constant vigilance. The body stays braced. The mind stays alert. The nervous system never fully settles.

When defense falls away, safety is often *felt* for the first time—not because the world has changed, but because internal resistance has ended.

This is a deeply paradoxical experience, and one that many people do not trust at first.

They wait for the other shoe to drop.

Defense Cannot Be Removed Deliberately

It's important to say clearly: defense cannot be forced to disappear.

Trying to eliminate defense is itself a form of defense.

Defense falls away only when it is no longer relevant—when whatever it was protecting no longer requires protection.

This is why insight alone rarely dissolves defense. And why presence, honesty, and non-interference are so powerful.

Defense relaxes when it feels safe to do so.

The Quiet That Follows

When nothing is being defended, something remarkable happens.

Silence appears—not as emptiness, but as rest.

In that silence, clarity does not need to announce itself. It does not need to be named or preserved. It simply operates.

This silence is not permanent.
It does not need to be.

It returns whenever defense is absent.

What Comes Next

The next chapter explores what happens when even self-support falls away—when there is no longer an effort to hold oneself together, improve, or stabilize experience.

For now, it is enough to recognize this:

Defense is not a flaw.
It is a signal.

And when that signal is no longer needed, clarity does not have to be sought.

It remains—quietly—when nothing is being defended.

Chapter 9
The End of Self-Support

"When I let go of what I am, I become what I might be."
— Laozi

There comes a point—often quietly—when something fundamental changes.

It is not a breakthrough.
It is not an insight.
It is not an achievement.

It is the moment when the effort to hold oneself together relaxes.

For many people, this moment is so understated that it barely registers. There is no drama, no announcement, no clear before-and-after. And yet, once it has occurred, something never quite returns to the way it was.

This chapter explores that moment.

What Self-Support Usually Means

Self-support is generally understood as something positive.

It suggests resilience, responsibility, and independence. It implies the ability to cope, adapt, and keep going. In difficult circumstances, self-support can be essential. It keeps life moving when conditions are demanding or unclear.

But over time, self-support often expands beyond necessity.

It becomes a constant posture rather than a situational response.

Instead of supporting action, it begins supporting identity. Instead of meeting moments of need, it becomes a background effort to maintain coherence, stability, and continuity of self.

This is where the problem begins.

The Subtle Burden of Holding Together

Most people are not aware of how much effort goes into simply being themselves.

Not effort in the sense of visible work, but effort in the sense of internal maintenance:

- regulating emotion
- managing perception
- sustaining motivation
- monitoring reactions
- keeping experience within acceptable bounds

This effort is rarely conscious. It feels like life itself.

But it has a cost.

The body remains slightly braced.
The mind remains slightly engaged.
Rest never fully completes.

This is why even periods of inactivity can feel tiring.

When Self-Support Stops Working

The end of self-support does not come from understanding.

It usually comes from exhaustion, honesty, or irrelevance.

Sometimes the system simply cannot keep sustaining the effort. Sometimes the reason for holding together dissolves. Sometimes the individual sees—clearly and without drama—that the effort is no longer doing what it once did.

At that point, something gives.

Not collapses.
Releases.

This Is Not Giving Up

It's important to be precise here.

The end of self-support is not giving up on life, responsibility, or care. It is not resignation, apathy, or withdrawal. Those are still strategies. They still require effort.

What ends is the *unnecessary* effort to manage experience internally.

Life continues.
Action continues.
Care continues.

What stops is the constant self-holding layered on top of it all.

What It Feels Like When Self-Support Ends

When self-support relaxes, people often report:

- a surprising sense of steadiness
- less internal commentary
- emotion that moves more cleanly
- effort that feels proportional rather than driven

There is often relief — but also unfamiliarity.

Many people don't trust this state at first. It feels too quiet. Too unforced. Too unguarded.

They look for something to do.

Nothing appears.

Why This Feels Unsafe at First

Self-support is deeply associated with survival.

For much of life, holding oneself together *was* necessary. It protected against chaos, rejection, or harm. Letting go of that effort can feel like stepping out of armor in unfamiliar terrain.

The nervous system may remain alert even after the effort has dropped.

This does not mean something is wrong.
It means the system is recalibrating.

Self-Support vs. Coherence

There is a subtle but critical distinction here.

Self-support is effort applied to maintain coherence.
Coherence is what remains when effort is no longer needed.

When self-support ends, coherence does not disappear. It becomes more visible.

Thought organizes naturally.
Action aligns more easily.
Rest actually rests.

This is not because life has become easier, but because interference has reduced.

Why This Is So Rarely Talked About

The end of self-support is rarely described clearly because it does not fit cultural narratives.

It is not heroic.
It is not productive.
It cannot be prescribed.

And it does not make one special.

In fact, it often makes one quieter.

This quietness is sometimes mistaken for disengagement. But it is the opposite. It is engagement without self-reference.

The Return of Simplicity

When self-support ends, many things simplify on their own.

Decisions feel less weighted.
Relationships feel less performative.
Expression feels less guarded.

This simplicity is not naïveté. It is clarity without maintenance.

Nothing to Maintain

Perhaps the most destabilizing aspect of this shift is the realization that there is nothing to hold onto.

No state to preserve.
No identity to stabilize.
No clarity to defend.

This can feel disorienting at first. But it is also deeply freeing.

Clarity that does not need support is remarkably resilient.

What Comes Next

With self-support gone, something else becomes visible: how life continues without being held together from the inside.

The following chapters explore the contexts in which this is most often discovered—not through effort, but through circumstance: grief, exhaustion, presence, love, awe.

Each of these reveals the same truth from a different angle.

For now, it is enough to notice this:

When the effort to hold yourself together ends, nothing essential is lost.

What remains was never fragile.

Chapter 10
During Grief

Grief does not arrive gently.

It arrives as rupture.

Something that was woven into the fabric of life is suddenly absent. A person, a future, a sense of continuity — gone. The mind struggles to orient. Time loses its familiar rhythm. Ordinary concerns fall strangely flat.

And yet, alongside the pain, something else often appears.

Clarity.

Not insight.
Not consolation.
But a stark, unmistakable clarity that cuts through noise without effort.

This chapter is about that clarity — not to explain grief, soften it, or redeem it, but to recognize what grief reveals when nothing else is able to interfere.

What Grief Removes

Grief strips life down quickly.

Priorities collapse.
Pretense falls away.
Energy once spent maintaining appearances disappears.

The mind no longer has the capacity to perform its usual functions of optimization and self-management. Long-term planning loses relevance. Narratives about progress, improvement, or trajectory feel hollow.

What remains is immediacy.

Breath.
Sensation.
Memory.
Absence.

In grief, the system no longer has the resources to defend, fix, or support itself. Much of what usually obscures perception simply drops — not because it is released deliberately, but because it can no longer be sustained.

This is not a gift of grief.
It is a consequence of subtraction.

The Honesty of Loss

Grief is brutally honest.

It does not negotiate.
It does not reassure.
It does not allow interpretation to soften reality.

Something has happened.
Something cannot be undone.

This finality silences many internal arguments. Questions that once demanded answers lose their urgency. Beliefs that once felt essential lose their authority.

In this silence, clarity stands exposed.

People often describe moments during grief when they suddenly see what matters and what does not — with startling precision. Small things feel intolerable. Certain relationships feel irrelevant. Other connections feel sacred.

This clarity is not wisdom gained through reflection. It is perception unobstructed by distraction.

Why Grief Feels So Raw

Grief hurts because it bypasses defenses.

Normally, emotional experience is mediated by explanation, judgment, and narrative. In grief, those mediations fail. The feeling arrives unfiltered.

This rawness is exhausting.
It is also clarifying.

When feeling is allowed — not managed, interpreted, or redirected — it completes more honestly. It moves. It breathes. It does not linger as distortion.

Grief hurts not because it is pathological, but because it is undiluted.

The Temporary Collapse of Identity

One of the most disorienting aspects of grief is the loss of identity.

Roles tied to the lost person or future dissolve. Habits lose context. The self that once navigated the world feels incomplete or unfamiliar.

This can feel terrifying.

But it also removes enormous effort.

Without identity to maintain, there is nothing to defend. Without defense, perception clears. The world appears as it is — stark, immediate, and strangely simple.

Many people notice that during grief they become less concerned with how they are perceived. Social performance feels pointless. There is no energy for self-image.

This absence of self-support reveals something essential.

Clarity Without Comfort

The clarity that appears during grief is not comforting.

It does not soothe pain or resolve loss. It does not explain why things happened or promise that everything will be okay.

It simply shows what is true.

This is why people sometimes feel guilty noticing clarity during grief — as though perceiving clearly somehow betrays the depth of their loss. But clarity does not negate love. It does not diminish grief. It does not replace meaning.

It coexists.

Pain and clarity are not opposites.
They often arrive together.

Why Grief Is So Often Avoided

Modern culture is deeply uncomfortable with grief.

It interrupts productivity.
It resists fixing.
It cannot be optimized.

As a result, people are often encouraged — subtly or overtly — to move through grief quickly, to find meaning, to reframe, to heal.

While support can be valuable, premature interpretation often reintroduces noise.

Grief resolves in its own time when it is not interfered with.

The clarity that grief reveals fades not because grief ends, but because life slowly re-accumulates. Responsibilities return. Narratives rebuild. Identity reforms.

This is natural.

What matters is not holding onto grief, but recognizing what grief made visible.

Grief as a Reference Point

People who have moved through grief often report a quiet knowing that stays with them.

They may return to normal life, but something remains altered. Certain concerns never regain their former weight. Certain truths cannot be unseen.

This is not because grief taught them something new.
It is because grief temporarily removed what was false.

The reference point remains.

Even years later, people may remember moments during grief when life felt brutally clear — moments when they could see without distortion what mattered, what did not, and what was no longer worth carrying.

Letting Grief Be What It Is

This chapter does not suggest that grief should be sought, welcomed, or used.

Grief is not a teacher.
It is not a path.
It is not a tool.

It is an event that reveals what clarity looks like when nothing interferes.

The mistake is not in grieving.
The mistake is in forgetting what was seen.

What Grief Shows Without Saying

Grief shows that clarity does not depend on comfort.
That meaning does not require explanation.
That perception sharpens when defenses fall.

It shows that when life strips us bare, what remains is not chaos — it is simplicity.

This simplicity does not solve grief.
It coexists with it.

What Comes Next

Grief is one doorway through which clarity enters uninvited.

The next chapters explore other doorways — moments when the system is exhausted, stilled, or softened enough that interference drops without effort.

Each context reveals the same truth from a different angle:

Clarity does not need to be created.
It appears when nothing blocks it.

For now, let this be enough:

In grief, nothing is being defended.
Nothing is being fixed.
Nothing is being supported.

And in that absence, clarity stands — quietly, unmistakably — alongside loss.

Chapter 11
After Exhaustion

Exhaustion is not subtle.

It arrives when effort has been spent beyond its usefulness. When the system has given everything it knows how to give. When there is no longer energy to maintain posture, narrative, or resistance.

Unlike grief, exhaustion does not arrive through loss. It arrives through persistence.

And like grief, it removes interference without asking.

What Exhaustion Ends

Exhaustion ends pretending.

When a person is exhausted, there is no surplus energy for performance. The mind stops rehearsing. The body stops bracing. The usual internal negotiations fall silent — not because they have been resolved, but because they can no longer be sustained.

This is why exhaustion can feel strangely honest.

There is no longer energy to be someone.
Only to be.

The Collapse of Effort

For most of life, effort is layered.

There is effort required by the situation — and effort added by belief, expectation, and self-management. This added effort often goes unnoticed until it is gone.

Exhaustion strips life down to what is necessary.

Tasks either happen or they don't. Words are either spoken or withheld. Decisions become simpler, not because clarity is sought, but because complexity is no longer tolerable.

This simplification is not laziness.
It is precision forced by limits.

Why Exhaustion Can Feel Like Relief

People are often surprised by the relief that follows exhaustion.

After long periods of striving, coping, or holding together, exhaustion can bring a quiet sense of release. Not happiness. Not peace. Just *less pressure*.

The system stops demanding coherence.
The self stops insisting on control.

In that absence, clarity appears.

Not brightly.
Not dramatically.
But unmistakably.

Exhaustion vs. Burnout

It's important to make a distinction.

Burnout is exhaustion combined with resistance.
Exhaustion alone is simply depletion.

Burnout is painful because effort continues even when energy is gone. Exhaustion resolves when effort finally stops.

This is why people often feel worse before they feel better. The system resists stopping until it cannot continue. Only then does the additional effort fall away.

What remains is raw capacity — limited, honest, and clear.

The End of Choice

One of the most clarifying aspects of exhaustion is the end of choice.

When energy is depleted, many options disappear. What remains is what can actually be done. This removal of choice reduces noise dramatically.

There is no debate.
No optimization.
No justification.

Action becomes simple because it must.

This simplicity reveals how much effort is usually spent maintaining optional complexity.

Exhaustion and the Body

In exhaustion, the body becomes unavoidable.

Signals that were previously overridden assert themselves. Rest is no longer optional. Sensation becomes louder than thought. The body dictates pace.

This is often experienced as humbling — or even humiliating — especially in cultures that prize endurance and control.

But the body is not making a demand.
It is stating a fact.

When listened to, clarity follows.

The Honesty of Limits

Exhaustion teaches limits — not intellectually, but somatically.

The mind may have believed it could keep going. The body proves otherwise. This proof does not argue. It does not explain. It simply asserts reality.

In this assertion, many beliefs dissolve quietly.

Beliefs about capacity.
Beliefs about obligation.
Beliefs about identity.

What remains is what is actually possible.

And that is often enough.

Why Exhaustion Is So Often Pathologized

Exhaustion is uncomfortable for others.

It interrupts expectations.
It refuses productivity.
It cannot be coached through easily.

As a result, exhaustion is often treated as a problem to solve rather than a condition to respect. People are encouraged to push through, optimize recovery, or reframe their experience.

While support can be valuable, premature intervention often restores interference.

Exhaustion resolves when effort ends.
Not when effort is redirected.

The Quiet Return

After exhaustion has run its course, people often notice a subtle shift.

They may still be tired.
Life may still be demanding.
Circumstances may be unchanged.

And yet something is different.

There is less urgency.
Less internal pressure.
Less insistence on being more than what is possible.

Clarity does not arrive as insight.
It arrives as permission.

Exhaustion as a Reference Point

Like grief, exhaustion can become a reference point.

People remember what it felt like when effort finally stopped — when nothing more could be demanded. They may return to striving later, but something in them remembers that clarity did not vanish when effort ended.

It emerged.

This memory becomes quietly protective.

Not a Prescription

This chapter does not suggest that exhaustion should be pursued.

Exhaustion is not a path.
It is not a practice.
It is not a solution.

It is simply another context in which clarity appears when interference collapses.

The lesson is not to exhaust oneself.
The lesson is to notice what exhaustion removes.

What Exhaustion Reveals

Exhaustion reveals that:

- clarity does not require energy
- perception does not depend on effort
- life continues without internal pressure

It shows that much of what we carry is optional — sustained only by habit and belief.

When those habits fail, clarity remains.

What Comes Next

Grief and exhaustion both remove interference through force.

The next chapters explore contexts where interference falls away more gently — through stillness, presence, love, and awe.

Each reveals the same truth:

Clarity is not fragile.
It survives collapse.

For now, let this stand:

After exhaustion, when nothing more can be given, nothing essential is missing.

Chapter 12

In Simple Presence with Another

There are moments when clarity appears not through loss or exhaustion, but through contact.

No insight occurs.
Nothing is processed.
No effort is made to understand.

Two people are simply present together.

And in that simplicity, something quiets.

Presence Without Purpose

Most interactions have a purpose.

They are oriented toward exchange, resolution, persuasion, or outcome. Even intimate conversations often carry subtle agendas: to be understood, validated, reassured, or aligned.

Simple presence is different.

Nothing is being sought.
Nothing is being improved.
Nothing is being defended.

Two people share space without needing the interaction to go anywhere.

This is rare.

And because it is rare, it is often deeply clarifying.

What Drops Away in Presence

When presence is simple, several things fall away at once.

The need to perform.
The need to explain.
The need to manage impression.

Attention is no longer split between experience and self-monitoring. There is no internal commentary running alongside the interaction. The body relaxes because it is not being used to signal anything.

In this state, coherence does not need to be maintained.

It already is.

Why Presence With Another Is So Powerful

Being alone can quiet the mind.
Being with another can quiet identity.

When someone is present without demand, the structures that normally organize behavior soften. There is no role to fulfill, no position to defend, no narrative to sustain.

The self that normally manages interaction steps aside.

Not because it is rejected — but because it is unnecessary.

This is why people often feel more themselves in moments of genuine presence, even though they are doing less.

The Nervous System's Response

Simple presence regulates the nervous system without technique.

The body senses safety not through reassurance, but through absence of threat. When no one is trying to change, evaluate, or extract anything, vigilance drops naturally.

Breath deepens.
Muscles soften.
Thought slows.

This is not psychological.
It is physiological.

The body recognizes when it does not need to brace.

Why This Is So Rare

True presence is difficult to sustain in cultures built around utility.

We are trained to make interactions efficient, meaningful, or productive. Silence feels awkward. Stillness feels unproductive. Being together "without doing" can feel wasteful.

So we fill space.

We talk.
We explain.
We fix.

In doing so, we reintroduce noise.

Presence Is Not Intimacy

It's important to be clear:

Presence is not emotional closeness.
It is not disclosure.
It is not bonding.

Those may happen — but they are not required.

Presence is simply non-interference.

Two people can be deeply present without saying much at all. Two strangers can share presence without connection or history.

What matters is not relationship.
It is absence of agenda.

The Relief of Not Being Managed

Many people report that the most clarifying relationships in their lives are not the most intense ones, but the quiet ones.

The people with whom they do not feel managed — and do not feel the need to manage.

In those relationships, thinking slows. Expression becomes more honest. Silence feels natural rather than threatening.

This relief is not emotional.
It is perceptual.

Presence and Expression

When presence is simple, expression becomes spontaneous.

Words arise when needed.
Silence holds when it does not.

There is no urgency to say the right thing, because nothing is being defended. There is no fear of being misunderstood, because nothing essential is at stake.

This is why conversations in true presence often feel unusually clear — even when little is said.

Why Presence Cannot Be Created

Presence cannot be manufactured.

The moment it is attempted, it becomes performance.

Presence appears when effort ends — especially the effort to be present.

This paradox frustrates many people. They try to listen better, be more attentive, or show up more fully. These efforts are sincere, but they often reintroduce self-monitoring.

True presence is effortless.
And because it is effortless, it cannot be forced.

When Presence Fades

Like all contexts of clarity, presence does not last.

Life resumes.
Agendas return.
Roles reassert themselves.

This is not a failure.

The point is not to preserve presence, but to recognize what it reveals.

When presence fades, what returns is not confusion — it is interference.

What Presence Shows

Simple presence shows that:

- clarity does not require solitude
- coherence does not require control
- connection does not require effort

It shows that when nothing is being managed, perception is naturally clear.

What Comes Next

The chapters that follow explore other gentle doorways — meditation, religion (through the mystics), awe, and altered states — each revealing clarity from a different angle.

For now, let this stand quietly:

When two people are simply present together, nothing needs to be held together.

And in that absence, clarity appears.

Chapter 13
Meditation and Silence

"Silence is not the absence of something, but the presence of everything."
Rumi

Silence has been sought for thousands of years.

Across cultures and traditions, people have turned toward stillness believing it would reveal something hidden, sacred, or essential. Entire systems have formed around methods for quieting the mind, stabilizing attention, or transcending thought.

And yet, despite this long history, many people who meditate regularly still feel unclear.

This chapter is not an argument against meditation.
It is an examination of why meditation sometimes reveals clarity immediately — and sometimes does not — even after years of effort.

What Silence Actually Does

Silence does not produce clarity.

It removes competition.

When external input reduces, the internal environment becomes more apparent. Thoughts that were drowned out by activity rise to the surface. Sensations become more noticeable. Emotional undercurrents make themselves known.

This can feel like progress.
It can also feel like regression.

People often assume that meditation should make the mind quieter. When it does not, they conclude they are doing it wrong. In reality, silence is often doing exactly what it does best: revealing what was already there.

Clarity does not come from fewer thoughts.
It comes from less interference with them.

Why Effort Re-enters So Quickly

Most people approach meditation with an implicit goal.

To calm the mind.
To stop thinking.
To reach a particular state.

The moment a goal appears, effort returns.

Attention begins monitoring itself. Thought is judged. Stillness is evaluated. Success and failure quietly enter the room.

This reintroduces the very interference silence was beginning to remove.

Meditation then becomes another form of fixing — subtle, sincere, and exhausting.

The Misunderstanding of Thought

Thought is often treated as the enemy of clarity.

But thought is not the problem.
Interference with thought is.

In moments of clarity, thought may be present or absent. It does not matter. What matters is whether thought is being resisted, followed compulsively, or defended against.

Silence reveals this difference quickly.

When thought is allowed without agenda, it settles naturally.
When thought is controlled, it multiplies.

Silence and the Body

Silence affects the body before it affects the mind.

As external stimulation decreases, bodily tension becomes more noticeable. Subtle holding patterns surface. Breath changes. Restlessness appears.

This is often mistaken for failure.

In reality, silence is revealing where effort has been stored somatically. The body begins to unwind when it senses there is no longer a demand to perform.

This unwinding is not peaceful at first.
It is honest.

Why Silence Can Feel Uncomfortable

Silence removes distraction.

Without distraction, unresolved sensations, emotions, and tensions become unavoidable. For many people, this is the first time they have felt their own internal landscape without interruption.

This can feel unsettling.

The instinctive response is to reintroduce activity — thought, breath control, visualization, mantra — anything to regain a sense of agency.

None of this is wrong.
But it does explain why silence is often fleeting.

When Silence Works

Silence reveals clarity when nothing is being demanded of it.

When there is no attempt to calm the mind.
No effort to achieve stillness.
No expectation of outcome.

In those moments, silence is not a state.
It is a condition.

And in that condition, interference relaxes.

Thought may continue, but it no longer argues.
Sensation may intensify, but it no longer resists.
Awareness remains open without strain.

This is what people often describe as "meditation working."

Why It Cannot Be Stabilized

Silence cannot be held.

The moment it becomes something to preserve, effort returns. The system begins managing itself again. Interference quietly resumes.

This is why meditation experiences often feel temporary or inconsistent. It is not because clarity leaves. It is because the conditions that allowed it have changed.

Silence appears when effort ends.
It fades when effort returns.

Silence Without Practice

Some of the clearest moments of silence occur outside formal meditation.

In nature.
After exhaustion.
During grief.
In simple presence with another.

In these moments, silence is not practiced.
It happens.

This reveals something important:

Silence is not dependent on posture, time, or technique.
It is dependent on non-interference.

The Trap of Spiritual Identity

For some, meditation becomes part of identity.

"I am someone who meditates."
"I am progressing."
"I am deepening."

These identities are subtle.
They are also heavy.

They require coherence to be maintained.
They reintroduce comparison and expectation.
They make silence something to earn.

When silence is burdened with identity, it withdraws.

What Silence Actually Reveals

Silence reveals that clarity is not produced by effort.
That awareness does not require management.
That coherence exists prior to control.

When interference drops, the system does not collapse.
It organizes naturally.

This organization is quieter than achievement.
Less dramatic than insight.
More stable than any state.

Letting Silence Be Ordinary

One of the most radical shifts this chapter invites is this:

Silence does not need to be special.

When silence is treated as ordinary, it becomes accessible. When it is treated as sacred or rare, it becomes fragile.

Clarity is not a peak.
It is a baseline revealed intermittently.

Silence simply exposes it.

What Comes Next

Meditation and silence are gentle doorways — but not the only ones.

The next chapter turns toward **religion**, not as doctrine or belief, but through the voices of the mystics — those who spoke not of accumulation, but of subtraction.

They, too, were pointing to what remains when interference falls away.

For now, let this stand:

Silence does not ask you to do anything.
It asks you to stop doing… a little less.

And when that happens,
clarity does not arrive.

It remains.

Chapter 14
Through Religion (The Mystics)

"If you meet the Buddha on the road, let him pass."
The Rose

Religion is often associated with belief.

Rules.
Doctrine.
Authority.
Explanation.

But beneath the structures that grew around religions, there is another current — quieter, more fragile, and far less interested in certainty.

This chapter follows that current.

Not religion as institution, but religion as *direct seeing* — as spoken by mystics who pointed away from accumulation and toward what remains when everything unnecessary falls away.

Where Religion Becomes Loud

Most religious systems eventually become additive.

They add explanations for suffering.
They add interpretations of meaning.
They add rules to preserve order.

These additions often arise with good intentions. They help communities function. They provide orientation in uncertain times. But as systems grow, clarity is gradually replaced by structure.

Belief becomes central.
Authority consolidates.
Experience becomes secondary.

This is where many people part ways with religion.

And understandably so.

The Quiet Thread Beneath Structure

Yet across religious traditions, there are voices that did not reinforce structure.

They did not build belief systems.
They did not demand adherence.
They did not offer certainty.

Instead, they spoke in paradox, negation, and silence.

They pointed not to what must be believed — but to what must be *released*.

These voices are often called mystics, not because they were mysterious, but because they refused to explain what could only be seen directly.

What the Mystics Shared

Across cultures and centuries, mystics returned to remarkably similar insights:

- That truth cannot be possessed
- That clarity appears when the self loosens
- That language ultimately fails
- That what is sought is already present

They differed in metaphor, culture, and expression — but not in direction.

They pointed inward by subtracting outward.

The Language of Subtraction

Mystics rarely spoke in instructions.

They spoke in negation:

- *Neti, neti* — not this, not that
- *Die before you die*
- *Empty yourself*
- *Become like a child*
- *Let go even of God*

These statements were not philosophical.
They were practical.

They were attempts to collapse the structures that prevent seeing.

Seeing Without Belief

Consider how often mystics redirected attention away from belief entirely.

Gautama Buddha repeatedly refused metaphysical questions, redirecting attention to direct experience.

Jesus of Nazareth spoke in parables that dissolved certainty rather than establishing it, often frustrating those who wanted clear doctrine.

Laozi warned that the moment something is named, it is already lost.

Rumi wrote of love as the burning away of identity, not its fulfillment.

None of these figures asked their listeners to accumulate understanding.

They asked them to *see*.

Why the Mystics Were Often Marginalized

Mystics were rarely embraced by institutions in their own time.

They were tolerated when they could be contained.
Celebrated after they could no longer disrupt.
Canonized once their danger had passed.

Why?

Because mysticism undermines control.

If clarity does not require belief, authority weakens.
If truth is direct, mediation becomes unnecessary.
If silence reveals more than explanation, power diffuses.

Mystics were not dangerous because they rejected religion.
They were dangerous because they pointed beyond it.

The Inner Sanctuary

Many mystical teachings use the metaphor of an inner sanctuary.

A place not meant to be filled, but cleared.

When this sanctuary is crowded with voices — belief, fear, judgment, obligation — clarity fragments. When those voices lose authority, clarity stands unobstructed.

This is not metaphorical.
It is experiential.

Mystics were pointing to an inner state where nothing needed to be defended, explained, or justified.

Why Religion Often Misses Its Own Core

Over time, the teachings that pointed toward subtraction were interpreted through accumulation.

Parables became doctrines.
Silence became scripture.
Direct seeing became belief.

This inversion is subtle and tragic.

The structure built to preserve insight often becomes what obscures it.

This does not mean religion failed.
It means religion was misunderstood.

What the Mystics Were Not Offering

Mystics were not offering salvation.
They were not offering certainty.
They were not offering identity.

They were offering release.

Release from striving.
Release from self-importance.
Release from the need to be right.

This is why mystical insight often feels both liberating and unsettling.

There is nothing to hold onto.

Why This Matters Here

This book is not religious.
But it is aligned with what mystics were pointing toward.

Not belief.
Not practice.
Not hierarchy.

But clarity through subtraction.

Mysticism appears here not as authority, but as confirmation — evidence that across cultures, people discovered the same thing when interference fell away.

The Risk of Turning Mysticism Into Belief

Even mysticism can be misused.

The moment mystical insight becomes something to possess, explain, or identify with, it loses its power. The language becomes decorative. The experience becomes conceptual.

This book avoids that trap deliberately.

Mysticism matters here only insofar as it points away from itself.

What the Mystics Leave Us With

When the mystics are listened to carefully, they leave very little behind.

No doctrine.
No system.
No guarantees.

Only an invitation:

Stop adding.
Stop defending.
Stop holding.

And see what remains.

What Comes Next

Having passed through religion at its quietest point, the remaining chapters turn toward experiences that strip identity without ideology — awe, love, altered states, and finally, integration.

But nothing essential changes.

Each chapter points to the same recognition:

Clarity does not belong to traditions.
Traditions sometimes remembered clarity.

For now, let this stand:

When religion falls silent,
what the mystics pointed to remains.

And it has always been available.

Chapter 15

In Awe

"The mystery is not a problem to be solved, but a reality to be experienced."

Søren Kierkegaard

Awe does not announce itself as clarity.

It arrives as interruption.

Something vast, beautiful, or unexpected breaks through the ordinary framing of experience. Thought halts mid-sentence. The self momentarily forgets to continue its narration. For a brief span, perception stands open—unfiltered, unprotected, and unconcerned with explanation.

In that opening, clarity appears.

Not as understanding, but as *silence with eyes open*.

Awe Is Not an Emotion

Awe is often described as a feeling, but it is more accurately a *disruption of scale*.

The familiar reference points collapse. What felt important seconds ago recedes. Concerns that dominated attention lose their grip—not because they were resolved, but because they no longer fit.

This is why awe can feel both humbling and expansive at once.

The self shrinks.
Perception widens.

And in that widening, noise drops.

When the Mind Cannot Compete

Awe overwhelms the mind's ability to interpret.

Language lags behind experience. Categories fail. The system that usually names, compares, and evaluates simply cannot keep up.

This is not a flaw.
It is the point.

When interpretation cannot keep pace, it pauses. And when interpretation pauses, interference falls away.

What remains is direct seeing.

Everyday Awe

Awe is not limited to mountaintops or cosmic visions.

It appears unexpectedly:

- watching a storm roll in
- seeing a child absorbed in play
- standing beneath a night sky
- hearing music that dissolves time
- witnessing an act of unguarded kindness

In these moments, the mind does not ask what this means. It simply stops.

And in stopping, clarity stands exposed.

Why Awe Feels So Clean

Awe does not demand anything.

It does not require response, improvement, or action. It does not call for belief or explanation. It simply presents itself and overwhelms the usual machinery of control.

This is why awe feels cleansing.

Nothing is being defended.
Nothing is being managed.
Nothing is being fixed.

The system relinquishes control because it has no alternative.

The Temporary Nature of Awe

Awe does not last.

The mind eventually reasserts itself. Language returns. Interpretation resumes. The self comes back online.

This is not failure.
It is function.

The mistake is not that awe fades.
The mistake is believing clarity left with it.

Awe does not *create* clarity.
It *reveals* it.

Awe and Meaning

People often rush to extract meaning from awe.

They explain it spiritually, philosophically, or psychologically. They turn it into insight, belief, or worldview.

This is understandable — but unnecessary.

Awe does not need to mean anything to be clarifying.

The moment it is explained, interference begins returning.

Awe Without Interpretation

When awe is allowed to remain uninterpreted, it leaves a subtle residue.

Not memory.
Not belief.

But a *knowing* — quiet, non-verbal, and difficult to doubt.

A knowing that:

- concerns are smaller than they appear
- perception is larger than thought
- clarity does not require control

This knowing often lingers long after the moment itself has passed.

Why Awe Cannot Be Pursued

Like all contexts in this book, awe cannot be manufactured.

The moment it is sought, it becomes an object of effort. The system tries to recreate a state, and in doing so, reintroduces the very interference awe removed.

Awe arrives uninvited.
It leaves without apology.

Its gift is not permanence.
It is demonstration.

Awe as a Reminder

Awe reminds us that:

- coherence does not require explanation
- perception does not require effort
- clarity survives the collapse of scale

It shows us what the system looks like when it is momentarily overwhelmed by reality rather than managing it.

What Awe Shows Without Saying

Awe does not argue.
It does not teach.
It does not persuade.

It simply reveals what remains when the self cannot keep up.

And what remains is not confusion.
It is simplicity.

What Comes Next

The next chapter turns to a context that is often misunderstood: **altered states** — substances, chemicals, and experiences that temporarily remove filters without understanding what they remove.

This chapter will be careful.

For now, let this stand:

In awe, nothing is added.
Nothing is solved.
Nothing is held.

And in that absence, clarity appears —
as it always has.

Chapter 16

Drugs and Altered States

"If you get the message,

hang up the phone."

Alan Watts

Altered states have accompanied humanity for as long as memory.

Plants, brews, chemicals, and rituals have been used to shift perception, loosen identity, and open experience beyond ordinary boundaries. In nearly every culture, substances were discovered that could temporarily quiet the mind, dissolve defenses, or expand awareness.

These experiences are real.
The clarity some people report during them is also real.

The confusion begins in how that clarity is understood.

What Altered States Actually Do

Altered states do not add clarity.

They remove filters.

They disrupt the systems that usually regulate perception — self-monitoring, narrative continuity, belief maintenance, emotional suppression. When those systems are interrupted, experience opens.

Thought may quiet.
Emotion may intensify.
Boundaries may dissolve.

And in that opening, clarity appears.

Not because something new was introduced — but because something habitual was bypassed.

The Mistake of Attribution

The most common misunderstanding of altered states is attribution.

People assume:

- *The substance created this clarity.*
- *This chemical showed me the truth.*
- *This experience revealed reality.*

But clarity does not belong to the substance.

The substance temporarily removed interference.

This distinction matters enormously.

Because when clarity is attributed outward, dependence forms.

The individual believes access lies in repetition rather than recognition.

Why Altered States Feel So Powerful

Altered states feel powerful because they bypass effort.

No discipline required.
No long practice.
No sustained attention.

Interference drops suddenly, often dramatically. The contrast can be overwhelming — especially for people who have lived under constant strain, defense, or self-surveillance.

For some, it is the first time they experience:

- mental quiet
- emotional flow
- unguarded presence
- perceptual openness

This can feel like revelation.

But revelation is not ownership.

Temporary Removal, Permanent Misunderstanding

The clarity revealed in altered states often fades.

The system reasserts itself.
Filters return.
Identity rebuilds.

This is not because clarity was false.
It is because the conditions that revealed it changed.

The danger arises when people attempt to stabilize clarity by repeating the altered state rather than understanding what it removed.

Repetition without understanding leads to chasing.
Chasing leads to dependency.
Dependency leads to distortion.

Why Altered States Cannot Teach Integration

Altered states remove filters, but they do not teach how filters form.

They bypass the very mechanisms this book has been examining — belief, strain, fixing, defense, self-support. Because those mechanisms are bypassed rather than seen, they return unchanged.

This is why people can have profound altered-state experiences while remaining deeply confused in ordinary life.

The experience was real.
The clarity was real.
The understanding was incomplete.

The Body Pays the Difference

Unlike other contexts in this book, altered states often leave the body behind.

Perception expands faster than integration. The nervous system is stretched without necessarily being supported. For some, this leads to confusion, instability, or difficulty grounding afterward.

This is not moral failure.
It is structural mismatch.

Clarity that arrives too quickly can outpace the system's ability to reorganize without strain.

Altered States as Accidental Demonstrations

Seen clearly, altered states serve one function well:

They demonstrate what clarity feels like when interference drops.

They show what perception is like without constant narration.
They reveal that identity is not as solid as it feels.
They expose the optional nature of many internal constraints.

But they do not show *how to live there*.

They point.
They do not remain.

Why Some Traditions Used Them Carefully

In some traditions, substances were used sparingly, ceremonially, and with great restraint.

Not to pursue clarity.
But to **confirm** it.

The experience was contextualized, not repeated compulsively. The emphasis was on what the experience revealed — not on returning to it.

When this context is lost, the substance becomes the teacher.

And substances are not teachers.
They are tools that temporarily remove resistance.

The Return to Ordinary Consciousness

Ordinary consciousness is not inferior.

It is simply layered.

The goal is not to escape it, but to understand it — to see how interference accumulates and how clarity reappears without bypass.

Altered states show what is possible.
Ordinary life is where it becomes honest.

The Quiet Risk

One of the quiet risks of altered states is subtle dissatisfaction.

Once someone has experienced clarity through bypass, ordinary perception can feel dull or constrained by comparison. This leads to a subtle devaluation of everyday awareness.

This book moves in the opposite direction.

It shows that the clarity revealed in altered states is available *without leaving* ordinary consciousness — when interference dissolves through recognition rather than disruption.

What Altered States Reveal Without Intending To

Altered states reveal that:

- clarity does not require effort
- identity is not fixed
- perception can function without defense

They accidentally validate everything this book has been pointing toward.

But they are not the path.

They are demonstrations.

What Comes Next

With this chapter, we complete the contexts where clarity appears through *interruption* — grief, exhaustion, awe, altered states.

What remains now is integration.

The final chapters turn toward how clarity lives *within* ordinary life — without collapse, bypass, or escape.

For now, let this stand:

If a state reveals clarity,
do not chase the state.

Notice what it removed.

Because clarity does not belong to the experience.
It remains when nothing interferes.

Chapter 17
Living Without Obstruction

Living without obstruction does not feel extraordinary.

That is one of the reasons it is so often overlooked.

There is no permanent stillness.
No continuous clarity.
No sense of having arrived somewhere better.

Life continues much as it did before — with responsibilities, relationships, effort, and uncertainty. What changes is not the content of experience, but the amount of resistance layered on top of it.

Obstruction ends quietly.

What Obstruction Actually Is

Obstruction is not difficulty.

Difficulty belongs to life.
Obstruction belongs to interference.

Obstruction is what happens when experience is filtered through belief, defended identity, unresolved holding, or the need to manage perception. It is the extra friction that makes simple things feel heavy and complex things feel impossible.

When obstruction is present, effort multiplies.
When obstruction eases, effort recalibrates.

Nothing magical occurs.
Nothing is fixed.

Something stops getting in the way.

The Difference You Notice First

The first thing most people notice when obstruction lessens is not clarity.

It is **proportion**.

Effort matches the situation.
Emotion matches the moment.
Thought matches the need.

There is less spillover.

A difficult conversation is difficult — but it does not contaminate the rest of the day. Fatigue is felt — but it does not turn into self-judgment. Uncertainty exists — but it does not demand resolution.

Life becomes more *contained* without being constrained.

Ordinary Days, Less Noise

Living without obstruction does not feel like living above life.

It feels like living *in* it.

There are still good days and bad ones. There is still momentum and rest. But fewer internal arguments run alongside experience. Less commentary narrates what should be happening. Fewer layers intervene between sensation and response.

This quieting is subtle.
Others may not notice it at all.

But the person living it does.

Action Without Self-Surveillance

One of the clearest signs that obstruction has lessened is action without constant self-reference.

Things get done because they need to be done — not to maintain identity, prove worth, or resolve unease.
Decisions are made without excessive rehearsal.
Mistakes occur without spiraling.

This does not mean carelessness.
It means absence of unnecessary monitoring.

The system trusts itself again.

Emotion Without Accumulation

When obstruction is present, emotion tends to accumulate.

A small irritation becomes resentment.
A moment of sadness becomes a story.
A flicker of fear becomes a belief.

When obstruction eases, emotion moves through more cleanly. It is felt, expressed if needed, and then it passes. It does not need to be interpreted into permanence.

This is not emotional suppression.
It is emotional completion.

Relationships Without Management

Relationships change subtly when obstruction falls away.

There is less strategizing.
Less impression management.
Less effort to be understood.

Communication becomes simpler — not because everyone agrees, but because less is at stake. Silence feels less threatening. Disagreement feels less personal.

This does not guarantee harmony.
It allows honesty.

Effort Returns to Its Proper Place

Effort does not disappear.

It becomes accurate.

Effort rises where needed and falls away where it is not. Strain becomes a signal again rather than a baseline. Rest actually rests.

People often notice they do less — and accomplish more.

Not because they are optimizing.
Because nothing is siphoning energy unnecessarily.

The Quiet End of Seeking

One of the least discussed shifts is the end of subtle seeking.

Not seeking meaning, purpose, or clarity as an ongoing project. These things still matter — but they are no longer hunted.

The constant background sense that something is missing dissolves.

This does not create certainty.
It creates sufficiency.

Nothing to Protect

Perhaps the most freeing aspect of living without obstruction is that there is nothing to protect.

No state to maintain.
No insight to defend.
No clarity to preserve.

Clarity comes and goes — and that no longer feels threatening.

When it fades, there is curiosity rather than panic.
When it returns, there is no urgency to hold it.

This Is Not a Finish Line

Living without obstruction is not an end point.

It is not a permanent condition.
It is not an identity.

Obstruction may return.
Noise may accumulate.
Effort may become strained again.

But something fundamental has changed.

The system now recognizes interference when it appears. And because it recognizes it, it no longer mistakes it for reality.

What Remains

What remains is not transcendence.

It is participation.

Participation without excessive friction.
Participation without self-violation.
Participation without constant correction.

Life lived more directly.

What Comes Next

The final chapter turns toward what remains when nothing is being propped up — not as conclusion, but as recognition.

There is nothing new to add.

Only one more thing to notice.

For now, let this stand:

When obstruction ends, life does not become extraordinary.
It becomes *available*.

And that has always been enough.

Chapter 18
The Performance of Self

This chapter is written with care, because it touches something tender… our children.

Not only our children.
All of us.

What is happening is not a moral failure, and not a lack of discipline, and not proof that anyone is shallow or weak.

It is something quieter.

A new kind of environment has entered human life—one that follows us everywhere, speaks to us constantly, and gently trains us to watch ourselves while we live.

And when a person learns to watch themselves before they learn to *be* themselves, something essential is interrupted.

Not destroyed.
Interrupted.

And what is interrupted is often exactly what clarity needs in order to form.

What is actually being shaped

Most conversations about social media begin with content.

What is being posted.
What is being consumed.
What is being influenced.

But the deeper change is not in *what* we see.

It is in *how we learn to relate to ourselves.*

Social media does not merely show us the world.
It shows us **ourselves as something to be seen**.

Measured.
Reacted to.
Ranked.
Compared.
Edited.

Over time, this creates a subtle internal posture:

"How am I coming across?"

When this posture becomes constant, it becomes background tension—so familiar it often goes unnoticed.

A child does not think, "I am censoring myself."
They simply begin to trim their own expression before it has finished forming.

A teenager does not think, "My self-worth is externalized."
They simply feel their sense of value rise and fall with signals they cannot control.

An adult does not think, "This is addictive."
They simply notice it is harder to stop than it should be.

This is not because people are failing.

It is because attention, when it is constantly pulled outward, cannot rest long enough to become clear.

The quiet training of self-censorship

There is an obvious kind of censorship that comes from outside.

"You cannot say that."
"You are not allowed."

Social media introduces a quieter kind.

It is not imposed.
It is learned.

It sounds like:

"Will this be misunderstood?"
"Will this be mocked?"
"Will this be ignored?"
"Will this cost me standing?"

So expression begins to pre-edit itself.

Not only posts.
Thoughts.
Feelings.
Curiosity.

A child's natural voice becomes cautious.
A teenager's forming identity becomes strategic.
Even sincerity begins to perform.

Clarity often begins as something unfinished.

A half-formed realization.
A strange quiet feeling.
A truth that cannot yet be defended.

If the environment rewards what is already polished, then the beginnings of clarity are filtered out before they can mature.

Not because the person is weak.
Because the environment favors certainty and spectacle over slow formation.

Self-worth and the external mirror

Self-worth was never meant to be built on applause.

Applause spikes and fades.
It teaches the heart to measure itself moment by moment.

Social media makes applause ambient.

Not occasional.
Not rare.
Constant.

Likes.
Views.
Comments.
Silence.

The nervous system reads these as social weather.

Children and adolescents are especially sensitive to social weather.
Their nervous systems are still forming.

So it is not surprising that worth begins to attach itself there.

A quiet bargain forms:

"If I am seen, I matter."
"If I am not seen, something is wrong."

This can happen even in loving families.
Even to confident children.

Because this is not primarily psychological.

It is physiological.

Human beings are wired to care about belonging.
When belonging becomes quantified and continuously visible, the system strains.

The result is not just comparison.

It is **constant self-measurement**.

And constant self-measurement creates inner noise.

Not loud noise.
A steady hum.

And like any hum, it is only when it stops that its cost becomes clear.

Why "addiction" is not a personal flaw

Addiction is often misunderstood as love of a thing.

But many addictions are not love.
They are relief.

Relief from boredom.
Relief from loneliness.
Relief from uncertainty.

Social media offers this relief in small, repeated doses.

An infinite "maybe":

Maybe this will interest me.
Maybe this will reassure me.
Maybe this will include me.

The nervous system learns:

"One more."

Not because the person lacks willpower.
Because intermittent reward trains attention very effectively.

This is not a child versus a phone.

It is a developing nervous system encountering an environment designed to keep attention moving.

Compassion here is not optional.

Compassion is accurate.

What disappears first

The losses are quiet. They do not look like crisis. They look like ordinary life:

Shorter attention.
Restlessness in silence.
Checking without knowing why.

But what disappears is profound.

Boredom.

Boredom is not a defect.
It is where the mind organizes itself.

In boredom, the mind wanders.
Sorts.
Digests.
Returns to itself.

When boredom is instantly filled, the mind loses its chance to settle.

Along with boredom goes something else:

The ability to stay with the first wave of discomfort.
The ability to let a feeling complete itself.
The ability to remain with "I don't know."

Clarity often emerges *after* that moment.

Not during stimulation. After it.

If nothing is ever allowed to finish, the surface never clears.

The grief beneath the surface

Many young people carry a grief they cannot name.

Not always because something terrible happened.

But because something essential is missing:

Privacy of becoming.

There is a time in life meant for awkwardness.
For contradiction.
For trying and discarding identities.
For being wrong without an audience.

Social media makes rehearsal public.
It makes experimentation permanent.
It makes the unfinished self searchable.

So caution replaces curiosity.

And something dims—not because it is wrong, but because it no longer feels safe to be unfinished.

Clarity and interference

Clarity is not a stance.

It is a condition.

Throughout this book, we have seen that clarity appears when interference falls away.

In this context, the interference is not only time spent.

It is the internal posture of performance.
The habit of facing outward.
The reflex to translate life into reaction.

If clarity feels harder to find today, it may be because we are rarely alone with our own minds long enough for them to become quiet.

Children especially are being trained out of solitude before they can discover its value.

Solitude is not isolation.

It is where the self can be heard without interruption.

Speaking to our children

If this becomes a battle, the child becomes the battlefield.

That helps no one.

Understanding changes tone.
Tone changes everything.

A parent who understands can say:

"I'm not angry at you."
"I see how hard this is."
"I know this isn't just choice."

"I want you to have a place inside you that no one can vote on."

This is not instruction.

It is truth, spoken without force.

And truth spoken without force can be felt.

What this chapter is pointing toward

This book does not ask you to fear the world.

It asks you to see clearly.

Social media tends to add:

More voices.
More comparison.
More interruption.
More self-monitoring.

When these accumulate, clarity is not lost.

It is covered.

So the question is not how to win. The question is:

What can be gently removed so the mind can rest again?

Not forever.
Not perfectly.
Not through punishment.

Just enough. Enough for a child to rediscover:

"I can be unseen and still matter."
"I can feel something without sharing it."
"I can be bored and survive."

These are not ideals.

They are conditions that allow the nervous system to settle.

And when it settles, clarity returns on its own—because it was never absent.

Closing

If you are a parent, you may feel a weight reading this.

Not guilt.
Care.

That is love.

And love does not need control to be real.

This chapter does not tell you what to do.

It helps you see what is happening without distortion.

So that whatever you change—if anything—you change from clarity, not panic.

And if you are young and reading this:

Your worth was never meant to be measured in public.
Your mind was never meant to be interrupted all day.

Your life was never meant to be performed before it is lived.

You do not have to fight the world to find yourself.

Sometimes it is enough to notice what is being added—so that something quiet can return.

Chapter 19
What Remains

"Truth is what remains

when nothing is being defended."

(anonymous)

When nothing is being added,
when nothing is being defended,
when nothing is being fixed, supported, or maintained—

what remains is not an answer.

It is not a belief.
It is not a state.
It is not an achievement.

It is simply **what is**.

The Mistake of Expectation

Many people expect what remains to feel extraordinary.

They imagine peace without interruption, clarity without fluctuation, certainty without doubt. When that does not appear, they assume something is missing.

But what remains is quieter than expectation.

It does not announce itself.
It does not distinguish itself.
It does not feel like an arrival.

It feels ordinary — and unmistakable.

One of the most surprising discoveries is this:

What remains does not need protection.

It does not collapse when attention wanders.
It does not vanish when confusion appears.
It does not disappear when life becomes difficult again.

It is not a condition that must be maintained.
It is what experience returns to when interference loosens.

Clarity comes and goes.
What remains does not.

At some point, the question that drove the search dissolves.

Not because it was answered —
but because it is no longer relevant.

The question was born of interference.
When interference falls away, the question has nothing to attach to.

This is not resolution.
It is irrelevance.

What Remains Is Not Special

This is important to say clearly.

What remains does not make one wiser, purer, calmer, or more evolved. It does not separate anyone from anyone else. It does not confer authority.

In fact, it often removes any sense of being special at all.

And that is its quiet freedom.

Life Continues — Undistorted

After clarity has been seen this way, life does not stop.

Responsibilities remain.
Relationships continue.
Effort is still required.
Pain still occurs.

What changes is not life —
but the amount of distortion layered on top of it.

There is less resistance to what is happening.
Less argument with what is felt.
Less need to explain experience to oneself.

Life continues more directly.

Nothing to Hold

Perhaps the most unsettling realization is this:

There is nothing to hold onto.

No teaching.
No method.
No final insight.

This can feel disorienting at first.
But it is also deeply stabilizing.

Because what remains cannot be lost.

The Quiet Confidence

What remains carries a quiet confidence —
not in outcomes, not in understanding,
but in **experience itself**.

Whatever arises can be met.
Whatever fades can be allowed.
Whatever returns can be recognized.

Nothing essential is at risk.

The Book Ends Where It Began

This book began by suggesting that clarity is not lost —
it is obscured.

It ends by showing that when obscuration falls away,
nothing new needs to appear.

What remains was never absent.

No Conclusion Required

There is no practice to take from this.
No insight to remember.
No instruction to follow.

If something here resonated,
it is not because something was added.

It is because something unnecessary fell away.

And that falling away does not belong to this book.

It belongs to you.

The Handoff

The examples in this book were never meant to be complete.

They were chosen because they were clear.

Clear enough to show something simple
without explaining it away.
Clear enough to notice what changed —
not in the circumstances themselves,
but in what was no longer interfering.

They were never meant to be followed.
They were never meant to be repeated.

They were meant to help something become visible.

Across very different moments, the same opening appeared.

Not because something new arrived,
but because something unnecessary fell away.

Effort loosened.
A belief lost its hold.
A defense softened.
A demand quieted.

And clarity — which had never been absent —
stood unobstructed.

Once this is seen, it no longer belongs to the examples.

It can be recognized in your own life.

Often in moments you did not fully understand at the time.
Moments that felt simple.
Or strangely quiet.
Or briefly whole.

Moments when nothing was resolved,
but something stopped pressing.

If you look closely, you may notice that clarity did not appear
because you tried to reach it.

It appeared because something stopped standing in the way.

This is the only truth the examples were ever pointing toward.

Clarity does not need to be created.
It does not need to be earned.
It does not need to be maintained.

It remains
when interference ends.

If this is now visible to you, there is nothing more this book needs to add.

You may begin to notice this pattern on your own —
not as a method,
not as a practice,
but as recognition.

The examples can be released.

The book can be set down.

What opened then can open again,
not because you search for it,
but because you now understand
what was never required.

Nothing is being taken away.
Nothing is being replaced.
Nothing is being asked of you.

This is simply the point
where the book steps aside.

www.ingramcontent.com/pod-product-compliance
Lightning Source LLC
Chambersburg PA
CBHW031445040426
42444CB00007B/973